Padlock Picasso

The Password Artist

Story by:
Lemi-Ola Erinkitola and Ruchi Sharma

Illustrated by:
Yuffie Yuliana

www.thecriticalthinkingchild.com/cybersafety

ISBN-13: 978-0-9899933-6-4

Meet Padlock Picasso : The Password Atist

The second character introduced in the Cyber City book series is **Padlock Picasso,** a talking padlock who arrives in Cyber City with a suitcase and very special paintbrush.

She immediately excites the children by showing them her scroll of password rules that she's written with her paintbrush.

The first character introduced in
the Cyber City book series is **Digital Dan**,
the leader of the city,who takes the form of a cloud.

He represents the cloud storage system
and teaches kids how the cloud works
and how to stay safe online through
engaging rhymes and pictures.

The third character is **Smartphone Savannah**,
who goes by **Savi,** takes the shape of a small,
exciting smartphone.

She comes to Cyber City to teach kids how to use
their smartphones responsibly. This is an essential
skill for young learners, who may find themselves
using smartphones at home, in school, or even
in unsupervised situations as the get older.

The fourth character introduced in the Cyber City
book series is **Appi Alex**, who takes
the form of a phone app.

He is best friends with Smartphone Savi.
His job is to teach kids how to choose
the best apps to download.

He also shows them how to use apps
safely, so they can have fun while they learn
(and their parents don't have to worry).

She bravely crossed the
ocean tide with a colorful
paintbrush by her side.

Holding a suitcase
in her hand,
she waved hello
to Digital Dan.

Padlock Picasso was
her name, and kids
at Cyber City
were happy she came.

She came to teach,
to inspire and even shock,
the kids when they meet
a talking padlock.

PASSWORD

Padlock Picasso was ready
to show and share all
the password rules
her paintbrush
created with care.

PASSWORD RULES

Picasso was going to
give the kids some clues
to password rules
they should always use.

ANAGRAM
CODE

PASSWORD CLUES

The very first thing she
wanted kids to know
was don't rush choosing
your password.

Take it slow.

RULE # 1

Choose something
difficult to guess,
but not too hard.

And always remember
your password is
the best safeguard.

RULE #2

4ET%1ge6
DOG
123456
CAT
QWERTY
JELLY22FI$H
ABC123456
BIRD
J98VT-$56

Don't tell anyone your
password, not even
your best friend.

This is very important
or it can turn out badly
in the end.

RULE # 3

Parents are the only ones
who should know it.

They can even tell you
what to use and omit.

RULE # 4

Use letters, numbers
and symbols
don't forget.

And if it's not
8 characters long,
it's not ready yet.

RULE #5

PASSWORD ****
ABC123456
QWERTY
123456
4ET%1ge6
JELLY22FI$h
J98VT-$56

In your password,
don't use an
ordinary word that
everyone already knows,
like cat, dog or bird.

RULE #6

And please
don't make them
the same as your
mother's maiden name.

RULE #7

Make them to be anagrams
or some other secret code.

Just remember, it must
never to anyone be told.

SECRET CODE
LISTEN ⇨ SILENT
TRIANGLE ⇨ INTEGRAL
ALIGNED ⇨ LEADING
ELBOW ⇨ BELOW
OBSERVE ⇨ VERBOSE
shhh

Passwords protect very
important information.

So think long and hard
and try to use
your imagination.

USERNAME
PASSWORD
******

Padlock Picaso was happy
with all that she shared,
because kids who listened
were well prepared.